Rivers
and Streams

Diyan Leake

Chicago, Illinois

Edited by Joanna Issa and Penny West
Designed by Philippa Jenkins
Original illustrations © Capstone Global Library Ltd 2014
Picture research by Mica Brancic
Production by Helen McCreath
Originated by Capstone Global Library Ltd
Printed and bound in China by Leo Paper Group

18 17 16 15 14
10 9 8 7 6 5 4 3 2 1

Library of Congress Cataloging-in-Publication Data

Leake, Diyan.
  Rivers and streams / Diyan Leake.
    pages cm.—(Water, water everywhere!)
  Includes bibliographical references and index.
  ISBN 978-1-4846-0448-9 (hb)
  1. Rivers—Juvenile literature. I. Title.

  GB1203.8.L44 2015
  551.48'3—dc23   2013039544

Acknowledgments
We would like to thank the following for permission to reproduce
photographs: Alamy pp. 7, 21 (© David Wall), 12, 22c (©
Matt Botwood (CStock)), 13 (© John Morrison), 19, 23 (©
WoodyStock), 21 (© All Canada Photos); FLPA p. 11 (Ariadne
Van Zandbergen); Getty Images pp. 8 (MyLoupe/UIG), 20
(Cultura/Colin Hawkins); Naturepl.com pp. 9, 22b (Robert
Thompson); Shutterstock pp. 4 (© WayneImage), 5 (© Josef
Hanus), 6 (© Xavier Marchant), 10 (© Nejron Photo), 15
(© rm), 16 (© Radiokafka), 17, 23a, 23c (© Irina Fischer),
18 (© Frank L Junior).

Cover photograph reproduced with permission of Shutterstock
(© Dmitry Naumov).
Back cover photograph reproduced by permission of
Shutterstock/© rm.

We would like to thank Michael Bright and Nancy Harris for their
invaluable help in the preparation of this book.

Contents

Rivers

This is a river.

Rivers are full of water.

Some rivers flow down to the ocean.

mouth

The mouth of the river is where it meets the ocean.

A river is like a waterslide.

Many rivers start in high places.

The water flows downhill.

The water flows into the
ocean.

Streams

Rivers are small at the beginning.
They are called streams.

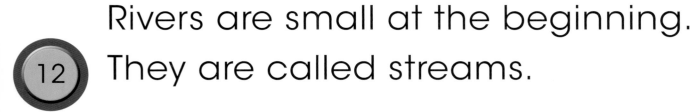

12

Some streams join together
and become rivers.

Rivers of the World

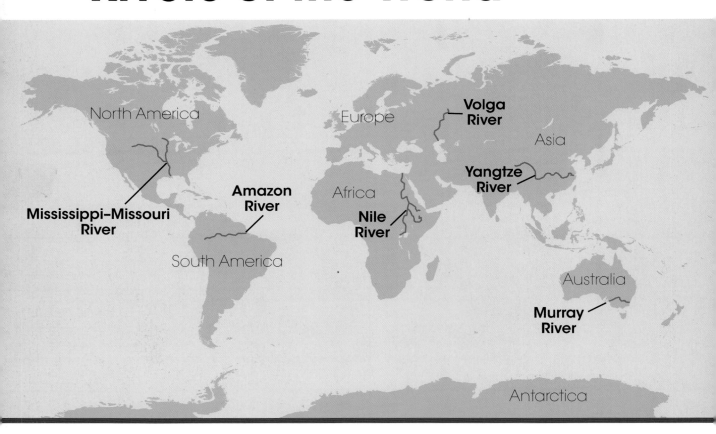

There are rivers all over the world.

The Amazon River is one of
the longest rivers in the world.

15

Boats on Rivers

16 This boat is on a river. It is carrying people from place to place.

goods

barge

This barge is on a river.
It is carrying a lot of goods.

The Power of Rivers

There is a lot of energy in the flow of a river. Energy is what we need to make things work.

River energy can be made into energy for our homes. It can be made into light and heat.

Having Fun on a River

It is fun to spend time by a river.

Stay safe! Always have an adult with you when you are near water.

Quiz

Which of these shows the mouth of a river?

A

B

C

22

Answer on page 24

Picture Glossary

 **barge** flat-bottomed boat used on canals and rivers to carry goods

 **energy** what we need to make things work

 **goods** things for sale

Index

Answer to quiz on page 22: Picture **A** shows the mouth of a river.

Note to Parents and Teachers

Before reading

Tell the children you are going to give them a clue about the kind of water they will be learning about next. Play the sound of running water in a river or a stream, using a clip downloaded from the Internet. What kind of water do they think they are going to learn about?

After reading

- Show the children how to make a "mountain" out of damp sand. Simulate rainfall by pouring water onto the top of the mountain. Ask the children to watch and describe what happens. Encourage the children to investigate further on their own.
- Reread pages 18 and 19. Explain that the energy in flowing river water can be harnessed by using a waterwheel. Show photos of waterwheels and water turbines. Help the children make a simple model waterwheel. Can they use the energy of water flowing from a faucet to make the waterwheel turn?